To:

From:

Warm Fuzzies

Compiled by Evelyn Beilenson

 PETER PAUPER PRESS, INC.
White Plains, New York

Photo credits appear on page 80

Designed by Margaret Rubiano

Copyright © 2010
Peter Pauper Press, Inc.
202 Mamaroneck Avenue
White Plains, NY 10601
All rights reserved
ISBN 978-1-59359-781-8
Printed in China
7 6 5 4 3 2 1

Visit us at www.peterpauper.com

Warm Fuzzies

Introduction

I n this cold and prickly world, warm
fuzzies can be hard to come by.
Here is your invitation, from our wise
and witty animal friends, to embrace
the comfort and happiness that is your
birthright. Dance to the music of your
own drummer, nap hard, listen deeply,

share the love, appreciate life, show up, flash some attitude, value play, have leisurely breakfasts, and adorn your day with hope, gratitude, and goodwill. From lions to lovebirds and from dolphins to dogs, furry gurus lift up your heart to the joy of the journey.

From small beginnings come great things.

proverb

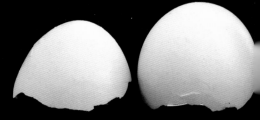

7

Music washes
away from the
soul the dust of
everyday life.

Berthold Auerbach

Am I not destroying my enemies when I make friends of them?

Abraham Lincoln

What a lovely
surprise to finally
discover how
un-lonely being
alone can be.

Ellen Burstyn

The more you
dress up the more
fun you'll have.
Brian Molko

Plants teach us about the human condition, what it means to be fully human. Pets do the same thing.

Judith Handelsman

Jumping for joy
is good exercise.

*Author
unknown*

I am happy and
content because
I think I am.

Alain-René Lesage

No day is so
bad it can't be
fixed with a nap.

Carrie Snow

There are shortcuts to happiness, and dancing is one of them.

Vicki Baum

Be a good
listener. Your
ears will never
get you in trouble.

Frank Tyger

Happiness is
not a station
to arrive at,
but a manner
of traveling.

Margaret Lee
Runbeck

When you come
to the end of your
rope, tie a knot
and hang on.

*Franklin D.
Roosevelt*

The first recipe for
happiness is: Avoid
too lengthy meditations
on the past.

André Maurois

Love is the only force capable of transforming an enemy into friend.

Martin Luther King, Jr.

It is a happy
talent to know
how to play.

Ralph Waldo Emerson

Moderation. Small
helpings. Sample a
little bit of everything.
These are the secrets
of happiness and
good health.

Julia Child

There is only one happiness in life, to love and be loved.

George Sand

To us, family means putting your arms around each other and being there.

Barbara Bush

43

In life, as in restaurants, we swallow a lot of indigestible stuff just because it comes with the dinner.

Mignon McLaughlin

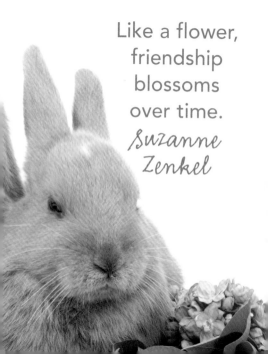

Like a flower,
friendship
blossoms
over time.
*Suzanne
Zenkel*

48

When you dig another out of their troubles, you find a place to bury your own.

Author unknown

Happiness seems made to be shared.

Jean Racine

Attitude is
everything.
—Suzanne
Zenkel

A good friend is
like a favorite book—
the inside is even
better than the jacket!

Sarah M. Hupp

Happiness consists
of living each day as
if it were the first day
of your honeymoon
and the last day of
your vacation.

Author unknown

Life is a short walk.
There is so little time
and so much living
to achieve.

*John Oliver
Killens*

Sharing
is loving.
Author unknown

All happiness
depends on
a leisurely
breakfast.

John Gunther

The nice thing
about teamwork is
that you always have
others on your side.

Margaret Carty

A bit of fragrance
always clings to
the hand that gives
you roses.

Chinese proverb

Too often we underestimate the power of a touch, a smile, a kind word, a listening ear, an honest compliment, or the smallest act of caring, all of which have the potential to turn a life around.

Leo Buscaglia

If you obey all the rules
you miss all the fun.

Katharine Hepburn

To love is to receive
a glimpse of heaven.

Karen Sunde

Happiness
walks on
busy feet.

Kitte Turmell

74

Bringing a child
into the world is
the greatest act of
hope there is.

Louise Hart

A joy that's shared is a joy made double.

English proverb

Photo credits